Linus Has Painful Tusks

By Clem King

Calum the seal went looking for his friend, Linus.

Linus was a walrus with two long tusks.

Calum found Linus sitting upon a rock.

Linus looked sad.

"Are you okay, Linus?" said Calum.

"No! My tusks are **very** painful!" said Linus.

"That sounds awful!" said Calum. "Did you hit them on a rock?"

"No, I just woke up and they hurt!" said Linus.

"I'm so hungry," said Linus.
"But unless I can fix my tusks,
I can not eat!"

"Wait here a minute," said Calum.
"I will find your mum."

Calum soon came back
with Linus's mum.

"You are a teen walrus, Linus,"
said Mum.
"Your tusks hurt because
they are still growing!"

"But Mum, I can not eat!"
said Linus.
"My tusks hurt too much!"

"A sore tusk is not difficult to fix!"
said Mum.
"Come with me."

Mum led Linus and Calum
to some snow.

"Calum, could you please help me?"
she said.

Mum and Calum pushed the snow into a big pile.

"Sink your tusks into that snow, Linus!" Mum said.

Linus sunk his tusks
into the snow.

He did a **big** sigh.

"Thanks for being so helpful, Calum," said Mum.

Linus pulled his tusks out and said, "Yes, thanks for your support!"

Linus was much more cheerful now.

He and Calum went for a swim and ate lots of fish.

CHECKING FOR MEANING

1. Why was Linus hungry? *(Literal)*

2. How did Mum help to make Linus's tusks less painful? *(Literal)*

3. How do you know Linus was feeling better by the end of the story? *(Inferential)*

EXTENDING VOCABULARY

walrus	What is a *walrus*? What do they use to help them swim through the water? Where do they live?
difficult	If something is *difficult*, is it easy to do or hard to do? What are other words that have a similar meaning? E.g. tough, hard.
cheerful	If someone is cheerful, how do they behave and feel? Are they happy or sad? What makes you feel cheerful?

MOVING BEYOND THE TEXT

1. Look at a map of the world that shows where walruses live. Why do you think they live in that area?

2. Would you like to have Calum as a friend? Why? Would he be a good friend?

3. Talk about how walruses use their tusks. Why do you think their tusks are so long?

4. Explain why the snow made Linus's tusks feel better. Have you ever put ice on an injury? Did it feel better?

THE SCHWA

a	e	i	o	u

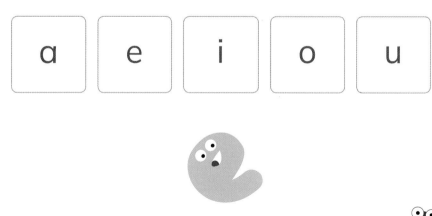

PRACTICE WORDS

Calum

the

Linus

a

walrus

painful

awful

minute

difficult

helpful

support

cheerful

A

upon

Linus's